Original title:
Melons in the Morning

Copyright © 2025 Creative Arts Management OÜ
All rights reserved.

Author: Olivia Sterling
ISBN HARDBACK: 978-1-80586-339-7
ISBN PAPERBACK: 978-1-80586-811-8

Fragrant Mornings

A slice of joy upon the plate,
Bright green waves as I relate.
Juicy laughter fills the air,
Nature's gift, beyond compare.

Bouncing seeds and sticky hands,
Sticky giggles, sweet demands.
Delightful chaos, a fruity spree,
Who knew breakfast could be so zany?

Refreshing Vibrance

Color bursts upon my tongue,
A festival of flavors sprung.
Juicy dribbles, sweet and bold,
Morning tales of fruit unfold.

With each bite, a cheer erupts,
Silly faces, giggles bust.
Beneath the sun's warm, glowing smile,
We munch and laugh for a little while.

Liquid Sunshine

A splash of color in my cup,
Swirling bright, I drink it up.
Sippin' smiles with every taste,
A sunny drink, there's no time to waste.

Gleeful splashes, laughter loud,
In this sweetness, I feel proud.
Every gulp, a burst of fun,
Liquid joy, we dance and run.

Heartfelt Harvest

Gathered friends beneath the tree,
Fruity bounty, wild and free.
Laughter mixes with sweet thrills,
In this garden, joy fulfills.

Wobbling bowls and silly games,
Tossing seeds—oh what claims!
A hearty laugh, a fruity bite,
We celebrate the morning light.

Tasting the Day

A slice of sun upon my plate,
Juicy bites, I can't be late.
Laughter bubbles, smiles abound,
Fruit parade, in joy I'm drowned.

Bright and yellow, green and sweet,
Every morsel a tasty treat.
Morning giggles, sticky hands,
Nature's sweets in sunny lands.

Nature's Table

On nature's cloth, a feast is spread,
Round and plump, they fill my head.
Sipping nectar, feeling fine,
Who knew breakfast could be divine?

Colors clash, a merry sight,
With every mouthful, pure delight.
In this place, joy knows no bounds,
Giggles echo, laughter sounds.

A Burst of Color

Splashes of green, a joyful hue,
Wonders waiting, fresh and new.
Chasing flavors, like a game,
Whirlwind of sweetness, none the same.

With every crunch, a snicker grows,
Who can stop when the fun overflows?
Painted sunrise on my plate,
Morning magic, can't be late.

Awakened Spirit

Awake and ready, I take a bite,
The day is silly, oh what a sight!
Sticky fingers, clumsy dance,
Each fruity morsel, a happy chance.

Giggles rise like steam from tea,
A bowl of joy, come dance with me.
Sunlight glistens, laughter peals,
This morning feast, oh how it feels!

Taste of Daybreak

A splash of pink and green delight,
Beneath the sun, oh what a sight!
A fruity feast, a morning cheer,
Laughter dances, summer's near.

I took a slice, it slipped away,
It rolled like laughter on the bay!
Chasing chunks in playful glee,
Who said breakfast can't be free?

Garden Dreams

In my garden, laughter grows,
With every slice, joy overflows.
A funny hat upon my head,
Wishing those sweet fruits were bred!

I shared a piece with a cheeky bee,
But it buzzed off, not wanting to see!
In flower beds, the veggies tease,
While I snack under shady trees.

Early Essence

Morning light brings a playful tease,
As I munch on sunshine with ease.
A neat little slice rolls from my plate,
Who knew breakfast could be this great?

A hungry squirrel seems to glare,
Stealing bites from my loving care.
I laugh and wave, share this delight,
While fruity giggles take to flight.

Essence of Joy

With each bright slice, my spirits soar,
A morning snack I can't ignore.
Juicy bites that sing and sway,
Brightening up this funny day.

A splash of juice upon my nose,
As I dance with what nature chose!
Giggles echo through the green,
What a funny morning scene!

Dew-Laden Delicacies

In gardens bright, with laughter wide,
A juicy gift the sun can't hide.
With fingers sticky from the thrill,
We munch and dance, our hearts to fill.

The dribble down our chin we weigh,
A fruit bazaar, a merry play.
Chasing each slice, a playful race,
With every bite, we smile and trace.

Orchards of Light

Under the beams of morning's cheer,
We gather fruit, the season's dear.
Splats of color on the ground,
A treasure hunt where joy is found.

Laughter echoes in the trees,
As we feast on sweet, juicy ease.
With every chunk, a giggle breaks,
In this garden, fun awakes.

Crisp Days and Sweet Ways

Beneath the blue, we chase the sun,
With every crunch, we're on the run.
Slipping on juice, we squeal and spin,
In nature's game, we all can win.

The juicy bites, a playful tease,
A riddle wrapped in joyful breeze.
With each sweet taste, a laugh we share,
Our silly antics fill the air.

Dappled Sun and Fruitful Dreams

In patches bright where shadows play,
We discover treasures, come what may.
With giggles mixed in every bite,
Our morning feast feels just so right.

We throw the seeds to see them fly,
While bees dance 'round and butterflies sigh.
Amidst the fun, our worries bloom,
As playful echoes fill the room.

Golden Glow of Nature

In fields of gold where secrets lie,
The sun laughs loud, the birds fly high.
A frolicsome breeze does shimmy and sway,
While chubby fruit giggles and plays.

Beneath the shade, a wild parade,
Ripe laughter bursting, a grand charade.
They bounce and roll with a cheeky cheer,
Each round little body grinning ear to ear.

The Promise of Pairs

Two plump delights in the midday sun,
A duo of joy, oh what fun!
Juggling their sweetness with great finesse,
Twirling and teasing—who'll win this mess?

With seeds like confetti and skins that gleam,
Together they giggle, a fruity dream.
Will you share a slice or take a bite?
They squabble and scheme with pure delight.

Lush Green Serenade

Among the vines, a choir sings,
The harmony of summer flings.
A chubby singer with a juicy tune,
Bouncing about, a merry buffoon.

In verdant realms where laughter grows,
Funny faces peek through verdant rows.
A crunch, a squirt, and all is well,
Each nibble, a giggle—come, do tell!

Sunlit Bounty

In the morning light, new joy does sprout,
Fruits caper around, there's never a doubt.
With wrinkled smiles and sun-kissed skin,
Cheeky and bright, let the laughter begin!

They bob and weave in the soft warm air,
A playful dance, with nary a care.
When juice begins to drip and flow,
The party ignites, it's quite the show!

Crisp Mornings and Sweet Flavors

With a crunch and a splash, the day starts anew,
Silly faces of fruit, all in a row.
They giggle and wiggle, a colorful lot,
Juice dripping down, oh what a messy spot.

Sunshine dances, bright and bold,
Slices of laughter, stories told.
The sweetness coats the air with a grin,
Cheerful bites, let the fun begin.

Bright Beginnings

In the dawn's light, surprises abound,
Fragrant orbs roll across the ground.
A game of dodge with a fruity twist,
Who knew breakfast could be such a list?

With a crack and a pop, flavors collide,
Wobbling charms on a joyride.
As giggles erupt with every bite,
Mirthful crunches are pure delight.

Afternoon Shadows and Juicy Delights

As shadows stretch and laughter soars,
Wobbling wonders peek through doors.
Splatters of giggles on sunlit cheeks,
Sweet treats dance, oh, what a feast!

Rolling chaos on a picnic spread,
Who knew these bright treats could leap like bread?
Chasing flavors, oh what a sight,
With each funny twist, we're taken to flight.

Whispering Gardens

In the garden where whispers play,
Chubby globes laugh the day away.
Teasing the bees with their happy hums,
Fluffy clouds giggle as bright drizzle comes.

In vibrant shades, they play peekaboo,
With cheeky smiles, they spring anew.
Every nibble brings a roar of cheer,
Such silly fruits, we hold so dear.

Freshness in Bloom

In the patch where round dreams grow,
A splash of color in the sun's glow.
They waddle like ducks through grass so green,
A jolly sight, a summer scene.

With stripes so bold and tales to tell,
Each slice a giggle, a juicy spell.
They bounce around like they own the place,
Showering laughter with every face.

Dune of Delight

Upon the sands where shadows play,
A fruity treasure brightens the day.
The ocean waves applaud with cheer,
As sweet juice drips, we bring the beer.

A party where the sunshine shines,
With laughter echoing in the pines.
These bouncing balls of sun-kissed cheer,
Bring smiles that last throughout the year.

Whispered Secrets of the Orchard

In cozy corners of orchard bliss,
Nature giggles, we share a kiss.
The secret whispers of vines so fine,
Each bite reveals a taste divine.

They huddle together, a patchwork clan,
With stories to tell of a sunlit span.
The crunch and the squish, what a funny feat,
As nectar dribbles down, oh what a treat!

Pathways of Flavor

Take a stroll on paths made sweet,
Where flavors mingle with every beat.
Bouncy paths of vibrant hues,
They beckon you with juicy clues.

Laughter dances with the breeze,
Each taste a jig, each slice a tease.
With giggles shared and smiles so wide,
The day rolls on, our joy our pride.

Breakfast Beneath the Canopy

Underneath the leafy green,
Lies a feast, it's quite the scene.
A slice of joy, round and sweet,
This breakfast is a tasty treat.

Squirrels dance and birds do sing,
As we munch on this fine thing.
Juicy balls roll with delight,
In the shade, what a sight!

Laughter echoes, crumbs abound,
Nature's gifts are all around.
Sticky fingers, smiles wide,
With each bite, our worries slide.

A morning that brings joy anew,
Ripe wonders, in sunshine hue.
Underneath the blue skies bright,
Oh, what a funny morning bite!

The Daybreak Feast

Up with dawn, a cheerful tune,
We feast as day begins to bloom.
Bright orbs stacked in a big bowl,
On this prank, we're on a roll.

Sticky juice drips down our chins,
As laughter bursts, the morning wins.
Fruits so round, they often tease,
Bouncing lids from gentle breeze.

A picnic spread, what a delight,
With every slice, pure delight.
The sunbeams dance on our delight,
Come share this morning bite!

With each round slice, giggles soar,
A feast of fun, who could ask for more?
In the light, with friends so dear,
This breakfast fills our hearts with cheer!

Nature's Plump Offerings

Gather 'round for nature's loot,
Fruits so plump, they make us hoot.
Harvest joy from fields so wide,
In the morning, we take pride.

Chubby treats and snacks galore,
With every slice, we laugh and score.
Tongues are tickled, smiles abound,
In the orchard, joy is found.

Jokes and jests fly through the air,
As we munch without a care.
Nature's bounty, bright and bold,
Warm sun kisses, love untold.

Beneath the trees, we share a laugh,
In this funny, juicy path.
Morning glows with every bite,
Oh, what a splendid morning light!

Sunlit Succulence

Rise and shine, it's time to eat,
Grab a slice, it can't be beat.
Sunlit balls, so sweet and round,
Joy and laughter all around.

In the garden, giggles flow,
With each bite, we steal the show.
Nature's bounty, life's silly quiz,
Who can resist this morning fizz?

Juice dribbles down, oh what a mess,
Sticky faces, who'd guess?
Rolling laughter fills the air,
A sunny breakfast, beyond compare.

So grab a slice, don't wait too long,
Join the fun, where we belong.
In the light, our spirits soar,
This morning feast, we all adore!

Lush Morsels Awaken

Round and juicy, what a sight,
Chasing critters, oh what a fright!
Dancing on the kitchen floor,
Who knew breakfast could bring such uproar?

Slicing open with a grin,
Juice drips down, let the fun begin!
A seed spitting contest ensues,
Laughter echoes, all the hues.

Morning rays light up the snack,
Rolling laughter, no looking back.
A taste so sweet, a reason to cheer,
You can't help but feel the joy here!

So here's to the bites, oh what a treat,
With each succulent slice, life feels complete!
In the chaos, joy comes alive,
Here's to the munchies that help us thrive!

Morning's Bounty

Sunkissed treasures on the table,
Ready to eat, if you're able!
Bouncing flavors, oh what a thrill,
Each bite's a laugh, it's never still.

Bursting juices, splashes fly,
It's a comedy, oh my, oh my!
Tipping over, getting sticky,
Life's little moments, oh so quirky.

Friends all gather, giggles abound,
Who knew breakfast could be so profound?
A fruity feast, a merry scene,
Who knew morning could be so keen?

As we munch and chortle away,
The day starts bright, come what may.
With each taste, smiles grow wide,
In the garden, we'll all confide!

Savoring the Sunrise

Awake with laughter, the sun is bright,
Breakfast jewels, oh what a sight!
With every slice, a funny sound,
Juicy splatters all around.

Gather 'round for a wild game,
Sticky fingers, but who feels shame?
Spritz and giggles fill the air,
Who knew breakfast could be so rare?

A pop of color, a taste divine,
With each bite, we laugh and dine.
Morning's joy in vibrant hues,
Skipping chores for sticky views.

So raise your forks, let's toast today,
To fruity fun in a bright display!
From gardens green to plates of cheer,
This breakfast party is our premiere!

Luminous Fruits in Bloom

Bright orbs gather in a bowl,
Morning antics take their toll.
Juicy laughter fills the air,
Who knew breakfast could be rare?

Poking and prodding, what a scene,
Splatting seeds, oh so keen!
Every bite brings silly sighs,
Morning giggles reach the skies.

Chasing crumbs across the floor,
Stumbling here and there, we explore.
In this mess, we find delight,
Savoring flavors, oh what a sight!

So here we are, a fruity troupe,
In this morning, we all regroup.
With each slice, let laughter loom,
Creating joy with every bloom!

Golden Rinds and Gentle Light

Sunshine spills on kitchen floors,
A slippery feast, a fruit that roars.
Giggles rise, a juicy spree,
With sticky hands, we feel so free.

Slicing through the golden skin,
Laughter bubbles, where to begin?
Seeds like confetti fly all around,
In this sweet chaos, joy is found.

Drips and drops from chins do race,
A fruity smile on every face.
Colors dance, a vibrant display,
Morning's bounty leads the way.

We crunch and munch, what a delight,
With every slice, the day feels bright.
Golden treasures, fun in each bite,
Who knew breakfast could ignite?

Morning's Juicy Gift

Wake and wiggle, greet the day,
In bowls of sunshine, we're at play.
Chomp and chew, the laughter swells,
With every bite, a story tells.

Sticky fingers, smiles that gleam,
A breakfast fit for a wild dream.
Slurping sounds, we spill and share,
A fruity mess beyond compare.

Sliced surprises, colors burst,
In this sweet game, we quench our thirst.
Giggles echo with every chew,
Who knew that sweet could be so true?

Joyful chaos, what a scene,
Bright and bold, like a daydream.
A morning treat, so fresh and grand,
In fruity wonder, together we stand.

Sweetness on the Horizon

Mornings glow with tasty charm,
Inviting smiles with fruity harm.
Splash of flavor, laughter's blend,
Each bite, a giggle, joy won't end.

Round and sun-kissed, glowing bright,
A juicy treasure, what a sight!
Seeds like spies on secret quests,
In each slice, a giggling fest.

Splats and smirks, we fill the air,
With fruity delight everywhere.
Trading bites and silly grins,
In this sweet game, everyone wins.

Morning's gift, a silly dance,
With each juicy bite, we take a chance.
Joyful whispers, the sun is high,
With every giggle, we touch the sky.

Radiant Orbs of Joy

In the kitchen, a riot starts,
With radiant orbs, we share our hearts.
Rolling laughter, fruit on the floor,
Slicing through jokes, we want more.

Bright bulbs of flavor, we all cheer,
Juicy bites bring contagious glee near.
Splatters of color, smiles to release,
In this fruity fest, we feel at ease.

Nibbles and chuckles, light as air,
Playing with flavors, without a care.
Who knew breakfast could be so grand?
With shining spheres, fun's all planned.

Golden waves of laughter rise,
In a fruity wonder, we seek the prize.
With every slice, our joy is shared,
In radiant orbs, we're all declared.

The Tapestry of Taste

In the garden of jests, fruits gather around,
Wearing smiles like hats, in colors profound.
One slipped on a peel, and shattered the peace,
Rolling like laughter, it never did cease.

A slice so divine, it talks with a grin,
Tickling the palate, it pulls you right in.
Jokes in each bite, a stand-up routine,
Fruit comedy show, it's a humorous scene.

The fruit bowl a circus, with juggles and dives,
Each piece a character, where laughter arrives.
A juicy performance, with squirt and with zest,
In this fruity revue, we truly are blessed.

Nectarous Sun-Kissed Bliss

Sunshine in a bowl, bright as can be,
A sweet little gem, doing a spree.
Dancing on forks, like it knows how to sway,
Whispering to taste buds, 'Come join the play!'

A pool of delight, with splashes so bold,
Dare take a bite, let the giggles unfold.
Squeezed in the morning, it's all quite absurd,
A tickle, a wink, oh haven't you heard?

Its laughter is sweet, sticky hands are the cost,
You'll know what I mean, when the flavor's embossed.
Wobbling and giggling, don't take it too serious,
This fruit's a true comic, all laughter, no furious!

A Morning's Melody of Color

A bowl full of color, a symphony bright,
Each slice sings a tune, a morning delight.
Harmonies of flavors, a chorus of cheer,
Craving the laughter as sunshine draws near.

A banter of sweetness, with notes of surprise,
Punny little fruits that dance and they rise.
Plucking at jokes, like the seeds from the inside,
These jesters of breakfast with nothing to hide.

So join in the fun, let your taste buds not frown,
Each bite is a giggle, come take a big round.
With every sweet whisper, the morning feels light,
These jesters of joy make our spirits take flight.

Crisp and Refreshing

Crisp and so catchy, a burst on the tongue,
Each nibble a story, where laughter is sprung.
A juicy performance, in each vibrant bite,
Drenched in pure laughter, delighted and bright.

Frisky and zesty, they dance on the plate,
Sliding and gliding, they can't help but prate.
With glimmers of humor, on sunny display,
This breakfast of glee, starts the day with a sway.

So come join the fun, take a fork, have a try,
These crispy delights, will have you flying high.
In the crisp of the moment, with giggles we chew,
Life's funny and sweet, take a bite, feel brand new!

First Light Feasts

The sun peeks over the hill,
A breakfast giggle, what a thrill.
With slices bright and juicy cheer,
A feast to start the day, oh dear.

The fruits are winking, saying, "Hi!"
On pancakes stacked way up so high.
A drizzle of syrup, oh so sweet,
With every bite, another treat!

So grab your forks and dig right in,
The morning fun is about to begin.
With sticky hands and happy grins,
The laughing starts, let the feast spin!

As juice spills down, what a sight,
This breakfast party, pure delight.
We'll dance with flavors in the sun,
First Light Feasts have just begun!

Soft Hues of Sunrise

The dawn breaks with a colorful show,
Soft hues painted for all below.
With fruits piled up, what a scene,
A kaleidoscope, pure and keen.

The oranges blush, the yellows gleam,
A breakfast fit for every dream.
In the sunlight, they twist and roll,
In every bite, a sun-kissed soul.

The laughter rings through morning air,
As sticky fingers are everywhere.
We make a mess, but who's to mind?
In the soft hues, bliss we find.

So let's toast our forks and raise them high,
To fruity laughter that fills the sky.
With giggles loud and joy that flies,
We savor life in soft sunrise.

A Symphony of Sweets

In the kitchen, a tune does play,
With fruity notes to brighten the day.
A symphony of colors swings,
Each bite a song that sweetly sings.

The berries dance, the melons prance,
Each flavor nudges for a chance.
A chorus of laughter fills the air,
As fruit and giggles make a pair.

Whisking up a sugary delight,
Honey drizzles, oh, what a sight!
With every scoop, a melody,
The sweetest song, come join the spree.

So let's compose a plate of cheer,
A fruity anthem, loud and clear.
With every serving, joy repeats,
A morning filled with symphonic sweets!

Nectar of the Gods

In the garden where sunshine spills,
Lies a treasure that gives us thrills.
Nectar flows from nature's grace,
A sip of joy we all embrace.

The colors burst in a zany way,
Golden hues for a brand new day.
With laughter bubbling all around,
In this sweet juice, pure joy is found.

We raise our cups to this delight,
A silly toast, what a sight!
The sweetness tickles, makes us grin,
Nectar of the gods, let the fun begin!

So gather 'round, let's all partake,
In this laughter-laden fruity bake.
With every sip, pure joy unlocks,
Celebrating life in fruit-filled clocks!

Ripe Radiance

In the garden, seeds take flight,
Juicy bulbs in sunlit light.
A squirrel dances, steals a bite,
Oh, what a funny sight!

Round and plump, the colors glow,
With stripes and spots, they steal the show.
A pig in shades of green and brown,
Rolls around, can't hold his frown!

Laughter echoes, the bees hum sweet,
Nature's treat, quite the feat!
Chasing shadows, all in glee,
In this patch of jubilee!

With sticky hands and silly grins,
We munch away, let the fun begin!
In this morning, so absurd,
Life's a canvas, won't be blurred!

Verdant Daybreak

Sunlight creeps through leafy vines,
Early birds begin their whines.
A rabbit hops, and then he trips,
He lands right in a bowl of nips!

With laughter loud, the creatures cheer,
As morning dew begins to clear.
Bees wear hats, quite fancy ones,
Flaunting style 'til day is done!

Fruit flies dance, a waltz in air,
A gust of wind, a little scare.
In this chaos, life's a game,
Not a creature feels the shame.

Glorious green, the day unfolds,
With stories grand, and jokes retold.
Nature giggles, join the spree,
A vibrant start, with joy and glee!

Morning Palette

Crimson, yellow, emerald bright,
A canvas spreads in morning light.
Critters scatter, chase and dart,
Each one's got a funny part!

The rooster crows, a blaring horn,
While squirrels clash, their acorns worn.
A bear trips over a wagon wheel,
Lands in sunshine, oh what a deal!

Colors splash, a wild parade,
Nature's jest, no need to fade.
Every laugh a brushstroke wide,
On this joyride, we all glide!

As we sip from cups so warm,
We crown the day, with nature's charm.
So grab a slice, and join the throng,
In this morning, we all belong!

Nature's Gentle Embrace

The sun yawns wide with a sleepy grin,
Waking up from nightly din.
A butterfly lands, rides a breeze,
And tickles a frog who laughs with ease!

In patches bright, the colors bleed,
A comedic twist in nature's creed.
A turtle peeks from its little shell,
And trips on grass—oh, what the hell!

The breeze tickles, the daisies dance,
While critters form a conga chance.
A snail joins in, with glee profound,
In this lush world, laughter's found.

Rollicking sounds, and joy's embrace,
Each creature wears a smiling face.
With every hiccup, every chase,
Life's a joke in nature's space!

The Palette of Pastels

In a field of hues, bright and loud,
The fruits wear crown, oh so proud.
With stripes of green, and blush so sweet,
They wobble 'round, on tiny feet.

A colorsplash on breakfast plates,
Dancing with joy, can't seal their fates.
The sunlight rays, they giggle and tease,
As fruits hold court with daring ease.

Juggling seeds, they spread delight,
Pink juice splatters, what a sight!
Laughing loudly, nature's jest,
These silly fruits, they know the best.

So let us munch, let's take a bite,
Pastel treasures burst, oh what a fright!
With every slice, a funny scene,
In this fruity dream, we reign supreme.

Sweetened Sunbeams

Bright as a laugh, a morning cheer,
Golden globes, they roll so near.
Sticky fingers, laughter rings,
Sun-kissed treasures, oh the joy it brings!

In playful splashes, color fights,
Drippy sweetness in morning lights.
All around, a giggle fest,
These cheeky fruits, they know the best.

Slicing smiles, a juicy jest,
Who's got the next, the very best?
The juice it drips, a merry race,
With sticky faces, who can keep pace?

Sunbeams spark, this fruity spree,
As every bite brings glee and glee.
So dip your spoon, join the fun,
In this funny feast, we've just begun!

Nature's Recipe

A recipe penned by nature's hand,
Silly fruits make quite the stand.
With giggling seeds and juicy spree,
They create smiles with fruity glee.

Whisk in sunshine, blend it right,
Laughter rises, what a sight!
Chop and slice with playful grace,
Nature's mischief we must embrace.

Sprinkle joy on every bite,
Flavors dance, a pure delight.
The silly chef, with apron tied,
Hosts a feast where fun won't hide.

Serve them up on plates adorned,
With bursts of colors, laughter scorned.
Each bite a giggle, fully blessed,
In nature's recipe, we are guests.

Morning's Embrace

As dawn awakes, the giggles soar,
Silly fruits burst through the door.
Bouncing cheer, with hues so bright,
They waddle forth in morning light.

With happy faces, they can't relate,
To breakfast plans, oh what a fate!
Platefuls of laughter, sticky sweet,
Dancing whimsical rhythms, upbeat.

Fruity hugs in glorious array,
Roll on floors, what a parade!
In every chunk, a funny twist,
A morning embrace, none can resist.

So grab a fork, dive right in,
Let juicy joy make your head spin.
With every bite, the laughter stays,
In morning's embrace, let's sing our praise!

A Symphony of Flavor

In the garden, bright and round,
Hidden gems can be found.
With colors bold, they call my name,
A breakfast treat, oh what a game!

I slice and dice with great delight,
Juices flowing, such a sight.
A splash of laughter fills the air,
As sticky fingers find their flair!

Sweetness drips from every piece,
A zesty joy that won't cease.
My morning bliss, a fruity song,
In this orchestra, I belong!

So grab a fork, let's dig right in,
For every seed, a cheeky grin.
With fruity giggles, our hunger's met,
A symphony I won't forget!

Sweet Dawn Revelry

Awake before the sun's bright ray,
I dream of treats to start the day.
In a bowl, a colorful heap,
Nature's candy, oh so sweet!

With each spoonful, laughter flows,
Splashes of juice, look at those!
Sticky hands and silly faces,
Morning joy in wild embraces!

The crunch, the squish, the vibrant hue,
I'm a fruity artist, it's true!
With giggles loud, I munch away,
In this sweet dawn, I plan to stay!

So if you're down, come join the fun,
With each bright bite, our joy just spun.
In the cozy light, we'll dance and play,
Revelry found in a fruity way!

The First Bite of Day

As sunbeams peek from sleepy skies,
I grab my fork and hear the cries:
"Dig in, dig in! Come taste the fun!"
The first bite of the day's begun!

Wobbling bits upon my plate,
The juicy treasures look so great.
I plunge my teeth with wild delight,
Sweet chaos sparks a morning bright!

With every chunk, a chuckle breaks,
Oh, the faces that I make!
A sprinkle of laughter fills the room,
As fruity goodness starts to bloom!

The day ahead, I face with cheer,
For morning bites are why I'm here.
So take a seat, come join the play,
In this feast, we'll laugh away!

Juicy Promises

Underneath a sky so blue,
A tempting treat, I swear it's true!
With every slice, a splash of cheer,
Refreshing joys that bring us near.

The flavors dance, the colors swirl,
As juicy drops begin to whirl.
Silly faces, sticky grins,
Amidst the giggles, the fun begins!

In this feast, we find delight,
With fruity tales to share outright.
Oh, what joy the morning brings,
In juicy promises, laughter sings!

So gather 'round, let's make a toast,
To all the flavors we love most.
With every bite, our worries cease,
In fruity bliss, we find our peace!

Shadows of Flavor at Daybreak

In the garden, shadows prance,
Chasing flavors in a dance.
A morning feast, bright and bold,
Whispers of sweetness, usually untold.

Silly seeds begin to shout,
In laughter, we twist and pout.
Nibbles of joy, a breakfast spree,
With every drip of sticky glee.

Giggles flow with every bite,
As shadows stretch and take flight.
"Is it fruit or a carnival?"
My taste buds cheer; I can't stall!

Together outside, we cheer and sing,
Contemplating all the fun that spring,
So come, let's savor this delight,
With every slice, the morning's bright!

Garden's Morning Embrace

In the dew-kissed garden realm,
Where laughter takes the steering helm.
Colors burst, a riotous sight,
A ripe surprise that feels just right.

With spoons of silver, we dig in deep,
Rolling giggles that never sleep.
A fruity feast, a slippery thrill,
As juice runs down, we fit the bill.

Petals laugh, and bees will hum,
While fruity wonders gently come.
Taste between laughter, that's the game,
In zesty bliss, we'll stake our claim.

So raise a toast to fruity cheer,
As sun smiles down, the fun draws near.
A morning joy that never ends,
In gardens where the laughter blends.

Slices of Serenity

On the porch, a platter waits,
Filled with joy, the morning's mates.
Slicing smiles, oh what a thrill,
In each bite, the heart can fill.

Breezes whisper sweet requests,
As we munch on nature's best.
Each juicy drip, a giggle sparks,
Like playful children in the parks.

Banter flows like rivers wide,
With every wedge, we cannot hide.
Sunshine dances on our cheeks,
A scrumptious joy that simply peaks.

So here's to bites of blissful cheer,
In every slice, we hold so dear.
With forks in hand, we laugh and play,
In morning's grace, let's bright the day!

Echoes of Dew and Sweetness

The morning calls with whispered tones,
As breakfast blooms on sunlit stones.
Chopping fun with every slice,
A sweet serenade, oh so nice!

Splashes of color tempt our eyes,
In this oasis, joy just flies.
Giggling as we chase the tastes,
Each drop of sweetness, no time to waste.

Bunches of cheer upon the plate,
A fruity revelry, it feels like fate.
Under the sun, we dance and play,
Whilst nature chuckles at our way.

So sip and savor, laugh aloud,
In this sweet haven, we feel so proud.
With echoes of flavors, we greet the day,
To sunny adventures, let's forever sway!

Rhapsody of Refreshment

In the fruit bowl where sunshine dwells,
Lurks a creature of sweetness, oh, how it swells!
Rolling like laughter, a jolly delight,
Slicing through mornings, a grand appetite.

Juggling with breakfast, oh what a sight,
The colors of summer make everything bright!
Bouncing with joy, a picnic awaits,
Whispering secrets to all on their plates.

A splash of the juice, a giggle or two,
Wearing my smile like sunshine, it's true!
Beneath a big sky, with friends all around,
A festival of flavors, laughter unbound.

So here's to the funny, the guffaws, and fun,
A dance of the tastebuds that's just begun!
Each slice a surprise, each nibble a cheer,
Morning's true magic is finally here.

Sun's Golden Caress

Awake with the sun and the bright, sunny cheer,
A round golden orb makes breakfast sincere.
With juices like laughter and textures so light,
Each bite is a burst of sheer morning delight.

Huddled around in a circle so grand,
We savor the sweetness, laughter unplanned.
With winks and with nods, we pass slices bound,
In the warmth of the morning, true joy to be found.

The critters all chuckle, they join in the fun,
As we chomp and we gobble, our journey begun.
The sun beams down, like it's tickling your nose,
A banquet of giggles, as everyone knows.

With smiles like sunshine, we bask in the thrill,
Each piece brings a chuckle, and laughter to spill.
Let's dance with the shadows, deliciously free,
In the glow of the morning, just you and me.

Sunrise Slices

In the light of the dawn, with a grin ear to ear,
We peel back the rinds, oh, what a frontier!
Each slice holds a giggle, a splash of delight,
The taste of the summer is just out of sight.

Beneath the bright canopy, joy fills the air,
With spoons and with forks, we all make a pair.
The colors so vivid, they dance on the plate,
Locked in a battle of laughter and fate.

Friends gather 'round with their spoons in a row,
As the sun paints the world, putting on quite a show.
A juicy explosion with every sweet bite,
We savor the moments, making them bright.

So raise a loud cheer, let the happy times flow,
With each playful nibble, our giggles will grow.
Sunrise, oh sunrise, you bring forth this bliss,
In every sweet slice, there's nothing to miss.

Dew-Kissed Rind

Awake with a chuckle, oh what fun awaits,
With nature's sweet bounty laid out on our plates.
A slippery dance as we cut and we slice,
The dew-kissed delight that is oh so precise.

A splash of green laughter, the seeds on display,
The taste buds unite in a fruity ballet.
Friends giggle and nudge, in this joyous endeavor,
For fun in the morning is bound to be clever.

Oh, what a spectacle, a colorful spree,
With every small bite, there's a new kind of glee.
Juices like rainbows, they splash and they spill,
With every new nibble, we laugh and we thrill.

So let's toast with our forks, to the giggles we yield,
In a bounty of wonder, our laughter is shielded.
With sunshine above and smiles all around,
Morning's delight is the best ever found.

Fruity Dawn Whispers

The sun peeks in with a grin,
A round green friend spins in,
Caught in a sticky, sweet embrace,
A splash of juice upon my face.

Giggling fruits, they start to dance,
Rolling around without a chance,
Dressed in summer's finest hues,
Who knew they'd make such goofy shoes?

A slice so bright, it takes the cake,
I can't help but laugh, for goodness' sake!
With every bite, a funny sound,
Like a trumpet in a circus round.

Underneath the bright blue skies,
Laughter bubbles as each one tries,
To bounce and roll, they all unite,
In this fruity morning delight.

Daybreak Harvest

Awake to find a bounty near,
Round and plump with joyful cheer,
The garden laughs, I hear them say,
'Let's make breakfast, hip hip hooray!'

A jolly splash bursts from the bowl,
A fruity dance that takes its toll,
They wiggle, jiggle, and then they splat,
I can't help but giggle at that!

With every slice, the laughter flows,
What a circus in my toes,
A fruity fight at dawn's embrace,
Who knew it'd turn into this race?

As sunlight climbs and shadows flee,
A funny feast comes joyfully,
The day begins in such a way,
With giggles echoing the play.

Juicy Dreams Awaken

In the morning, dreams still cling,
With fruity whispers, giggles ring,
A splash of sweetness on my plate,
A comic twist—it's just too great!

Bouncing balls of clashing hues,
Dancing round like playful blues,
Each bite brings laughter, what a shock,
Splattering juice, a fruity rock!

I swear I saw a slice take flight,
With sprinkles dancing, what a sight!
A trio forms, they share a laugh,
Half the fun is in the math!

So let the daybreak bring its cheer,
With fruity smiles that persevere,
A funny feast, let's share a toast,
To waking dreams we love the most.

Morning's Sweet Nectar

As dawn breaks with a giggling cheer,
The harvest spread, oh what a cheer!
Sweet nectar spills like morning light,
In a comedy of taste, a funny sight.

The fruit parade rolls down the way,
Colored laughter brightens the day,
Squishy, squashy, who'd have guessed,
Life's most funny in the zest!

A splash of juice, a squawk and squeak,
A funny face with every tweak,
They charm my taste buds, one by one,
In this silly race, it's all in fun!

So toast the morning, dance along,
With fruity puns, we can't go wrong,
A laughter feast, our spirits soar,
In sweet delight, forevermore!

The Essence of Early Hours

With a sunbeam's tickle on my nose,
The day begins with a silly pose.
A fruit parade starts to roll,
As laughter spills from my happy soul.

The kitchen's bustling like a zoo,
Sticky fingers trying something new.
Jugs of juice and giggles collide,
While breakfast plans start to slide.

A cat jumps up and swipes a slice,
The toast pops up—oh, isn't life nice?
Chasing crumbs, the puppy's in gear,
Dancing about, full of cheer!

Morning mischief, what a delight,
A symphony of joy takes flight.
With every bite and every laugh,
The day's perfect, on our behalf.

Slices of Serenity

Beneath the sun, we take our stands,
Juggling fruit and breakfast plans.
Sticky sweetness on our hands,
As we munch in playful bands.

Sneaky squirrels skitter and dash,
For a slice, they make a splash.
Giggles burst, amidst the fun,
Lemonade and laughter run.

Plates are filled, a colorful sight,
Each bite brings such pure delight.
A toddler's grin, pure and wide,
As jelly dribbles down his side.

With each soft bite, the world's a stage,
The morning's joy, a fun-filled page.
With fruit in hand, we join the dance,
In silliness, we take our chance.

Warmth of the Earth

The earth awakens with a yawn,
Golden rays spill on the lawn.
With baskets brimming, we all partake,
In juicy bites that make us shake.

A picnic spread beneath the trees,
Fragrant breezes whisper with ease.
Bites so bold and laughs so sweet,
With every crunch, we dance on our feet.

The puppy leaps, claiming a prize,
Caught in antics, he dreamily sighs.
A slice escapes to roll away,
Chasing joy in the light of day.

With whispered secrets as we chew,
The freshness of the earth shines through.
In every bite, life's colors blend,
A humorous start that has no end.

Encounters with Dawn

At dawn, the world is filled with cheer,
Silly hats and fruit appear.
Rushing to grab a tasty slice,
The morning burst is oh so nice!

A dropped spoon bounces across the floor,
Cereal spills, but who keeps score?
As giggles echo through the hall,
The kitchen's mayhem charms us all.

Butter's dancing on the bread,
Dancing shadows where we tread.
The day unfolds, bright and absurd,
With laughs and joy, it's truly preferred.

With smiles and fruit, our hearts delight,
Our silly morning takes grand flight.
In every crumb, we find our glee,
Through dawn's embrace, we're wild and free!

Cheerful Reflections

The sun peeks in with a grin,
Juggling fruit on a whim,
A slice of joy on the plate,
Giggling shadows, a merry fate.

Buzzing bees join the cheer,
As we munch without a fear,
Sticky hands, and laughter loud,
We wear our fruity crown, oh proud!

Tiny seeds bounce all around,
Like little confetti, joy unbound,
With every bite, a chuckle grows,
A fruity circus, oh how it glows!

Rolling seeds on the floor,
A playful mess, we want more,
Every slice brings a happy tease,
Smiling faces, just like bees.

Morning Glow

The dawn dances with bright hues,
Fruits giggle in sunny views,
Bouncing rings of zest so free,
Like little suns, they tease with glee.

Pies and juices all combine,
As we toast with a fruity vine,
Witty jokes and laughs align,
Morning bliss, a lively sign.

A playful chase to catch a slice,
In the kitchen, oh so nice,
With every drip, a comic show,
It's a carnival, don't you know?

Chortles echo, pure delight,
As we munch with all our might,
A breakfast dance in fruity bliss,
Wrapped in laughter's warm embrace.

Sweet Sunshine Symphony

In the morn when colors shine,
A fruity feast feels divine,
Giggles bounce like fireflies,
In each slice, joy never lies.

Maybe we'll wear hats of rind,
Just to see what we might find,
As laughter spills from every core,
Fruity tunes that we adore.

A rolling fruit race, oh what fun,
Who knew breakfast could be a run?
With zesty jokes on every plate,
Mirth and munching, just so great!

Hilarious bites, oh what a scene,
Chasing sweetness, like a dream,
With every chuckle, a burst of sun,
In this fruity fest, we're all just one.

Day's Early Blessing

Wake-up calls of colored cheer,
With fruity fun, let's persevere,
Balmy moments, bright and wild,
Glee of nature, pure and styled.

Chop, chop, giggles in the air,
As breakfast plays without a care,
With each cut, a joke appears,
Who knew fruit could bring such cheers?

Little hands grab every slice,
In the dance of sweetness nice,
Every munch, a funny note,
A giggling band, we're on a float!

Laughter sprinkles like the dew,
As we savor every hue,
In our hearts, this joy will stay,
Thankful for the fruity play.

The Taste of New Beginnings

A round ball of green, it rolls away,
Chasing shadows, not a serious play.
Caught in a patch, I slip and fall,
Laughter erupts; it's a fruit brawl!

In every slice, a hint of surprise,
Sugar and sunshine dance in my eyes.
Juices drip down, what a sticky fate,
I'll take a large bite, it's never too late!

Seeds spitting left, a fruity cannon,
By this delight, I'm totally driven.
A morning feast that's full of cheer,
Who knew breakfast would turn so dear?

So let the laughter fill the air,
In every giggle, a juicy affair.
With each juicy bite, I find a thrill,
New beginnings served on a breakfast grill!

Savoring Sunshine

Golden spheres shining nice and bright,
They tease my taste buds, oh what a sight!
Dancing with joy upon my plate,
Each slice whispers, "Oh, let's celebrate!"

Laughter bubbles like a fizzy drink,
Who knew golden orbs could make me think?
A fork in hand, I take a stab,
What's next? A giggle or a drab?

Sunshine sweet, not a worry in sight,
Every bite brings a glimmer of light.
I giggle aloud, spill juice on my chin,
Savoring the laughter, I'll take a win!

A plate of joy to kickstart my day,
With each vibrant slice, worries decay.
Bright morning bliss in every bite,
Savoring sunshine, what pure delight!

Aromas of Dawn

In the morning air, what do I smell?
A fruity perfume, casting a spell.
Whispers of sweetness fill my nose,
I think of a feast, as laughter grows.

Rolling in laughter, a fruit parade,
A symphony of colors in the shade.
With seeds as confetti and juice as cheer,
These are the mornings I hold dear!

Bright greens and yellows make quite the scene,
A zesty canvas, a breakfast dream.
With each fragrant waft, I burst into glee,
A festival of flavors beckoning me!

So here comes the sunshine, all bright and bold,
With laughter and sweetness, let the day unfold.
Aromas of dawn leading the way,
In this fruity fiesta, I play all day!

The Color of Awakening

Awake to a riot of colors so loud,
Crimson, green bursts, they make me proud.
They jump on my plate with a wink and a grin,
Inviting me over; let the fun begin!

Fruits launch a chat about who's the best,
With seeds as their jokes, it's quite the fest.
I take a big bite, it's a glorious mess,
Juicy laughter flows, nothing less!

A rainbow of sweetness, a carnival treat,
Dancing on my tongue, it can't be beat.
With every morsel, my worries fly,
In this fruity chaos, I can't help but sigh!

The day comes alive in a vibrant spree,
What a riot of colors, just fruit and me.
The color of awakening brings delight,
In this playful breakfast, everything feels right!

Juicy Awakening

In the kitchen, a slip and a slide,
A fruit on the floor, oh what a ride!
With seeds in my hair and juice on my shirt,
I laugh at the mess, it's all just dessert.

The sun peeks in, plays tag with my cat,
She jumps on the counter, and then there's a splat!
The scent of the sweet one fills up the air,
Who knew breakfast chaos could be such a flair?

Slice after slice, they're all in my dreams,
A feast on the table, or so it seems.
With bites of the sunshine, I giggle and cheer,
This quirky fruit feast gives me plenty of cheer.

So here's to the mornings, all juicy and bright,
With laughter and fruit, it's pure delight.
Slip on the peel, let the day come alive,
In this playful kitchen, I joyfully thrive.

Blissful Morn

The rooster forgot to crow this fine day,
He's munching on sweetness, so what can I say?
I trip on a peel while I'm reaching for more,
And maybe that's why my shoes stick to the floor.

Sliced up and served, the sunshine glows,
But watch out for seeds that dance on your toes!
A splash on my face, a giggle escapes,
Mornings are wacky with fruity capes.

At the end of the table, a fruit salad waits,
It's a jungle of colors, making me gapes.
With laughter and bites and a smile so wide,
Each chuckle I share makes my worries subside.

So let's raise a toast to this sticky sweet feast,
Where fun is the flavor, and laughter's increased.
The blender's now dancing, the fruit flies are bold,
In this wacky morning, all tales are retold.

Garden of Wishes

Out in the garden, what a sight to see,
Funny little shapes, waving back at me.
With spots and stripes, they jive in the breeze,
And beckon me closer with silly hand squeeze.

A hop and a skip, as I gather them right,
My basket's all wobbly, oh what a sight!
A giggle escapes as I slip on the ground,
The squash roll away, not a care all around.

The neighbors peek out with curious eyes,
Amidst all the laughter, time just flies.
I dance with the fruits, they twirl like dreams,
In a garden of wishes, nothing's as it seems.

So here's to the mornings filled with delight,
In this whimsical garden, everything's bright.
With juicy hoorays and a day filled with cheer,
We'll savor the giggles that spring up each year.

The Day's First Palette

The first light of dawn spills color so bold,
On a canvas of fruit, brighter treasures unfold.
With pinks and with greens, oh such quirky hues,
I dive into breakfast adorned with my muse.

A splash of confusion, the spoon met a pear,
It wobbled away like it just didn't care.
Squished by my giggles, the fruit takes a stand,
In this zany buffet, I'm in fruit wonderland.

A swirl of the flavors, they paint up the plate,
With chaos and laughter, I celebrate fate.
Each bite is a brushstroke, each smile a ray,
As breakfast becomes my most colorful play.

So here's to the mornings where fun takes the lead,
In this party of fruits, there's no room for greed.
Let laughter be vibrant, and joy share the space,
In this day's first palette, let's all find our place.

Sunrise Slices

A round and jolly orb in my bowl,
Wobbly joy that's good for the soul.
I lift my spoon with a silly grin,
Splash of juice, let the laughter begin!

Friends gather 'round for a fruity feast,
Chasing the blues, our spirits released.
Peels flying high, oh what a sight!
Who knew breakfast could be such delight?

Bite after bite, it's a juicy game,
Sticky fingers, but we feel no shame.
Giggles erupt with every soft splash,
It's a morning dance with a cheeky flash!

As sunlight pours, our worries fade,
In this fruit kingdom, we've got it made.
So grab a slice, take a big chance,
Mornings like this make the heart dance!

Dew-kissed Delights

At dawn they shimmer, a colorful crew,
Dew-kissed gems, each with a view.
Rolling in laughter, from tree to grass,
Nature's candy, we're having a blast!

Chomp on the sweetness, juice will erupt,
Faces all sticky and laughter is cupped.
Who knew that breakfast could be a thrill?
In this fruity chaos, we've found our fill!

Bright green and golden, they bounce and play,
High on our giggles, we savor the day.
A silly crunch turns serious strides,
Watch your step! Here joy resides!

So come one, come all, to this festival fun,
A fruit party grand, where no one's outdone.
Dew-kissed delights in this vibrant spree,
More laughter, more joy, just you wait and see!

Harvest Hues at Dawn

The first light breaks, colors galore,
Reds and greens rolling out by the score.
Giggles and grins as we harvest the cheer,
Snack time looms, and the fun is near!

In baskets we gather all shapes and sizes,
Each bite a treasure, full of surprises.
Slicing them up with a dash of flair,
Laughter erupts, floating high in the air!

With spoons in hand, it's a playful race,
Spitting the seeds? Now that's our base.
Watch out! Here comes the seed-spitting champ,
Bright morning colors, oh how they stamp!

So raise your slice high, let the fun unfold,
In this zesty banquet, watch the stories told.
Harvest hues at dawn, a riotous quest,
Join our fruity laughter, it's simply the best!

Fruity Whispers

In the sun's warm glow, secrets confide,
Whispers of flavor, we cannot hide.
A giggle, a crumb—what a funny sight,
Munching on fruits feels perfectly right!

They chatter and bounce, these slices so bright,
Each succulent bite a delight in the light.
With every crunch comes a chorus of glee,
A fruity fiesta, come join in with me!

Laughter cascades like a sweet summer stream,
Sharing these moments, oh how they beam!
In this playful dance, with juice on our chins,
Fruity whispers grow loud as the fun begins!

So raise your fork high, let the giggles fly,
In a world made of sweetness, we can't deny.
With each bright slice and every glad cheer,
Fruity whispers, oh sweet joy, let's hear!

Sunrise Melodies

Morning sun begins to rise,
The garden wakes with playful sighs.
Juicy orbs in green attire,
Whisper tales of sweet desire.

A critter hops, it makes a dash,
To claim a prize in nature's stash.
With each bite, a giggle bursts,
As juice dribbles, oh how it thirsts!

Birds join in, they chirp and cheer,
While sticky fingers bring us near.
Laughter fills the air so bright,
As fruit-filled joy takes flight tonight.

Summer's First Crush

A fruity fling beneath the sky,
Sweetness makes us laugh and sigh.
Dressed in smiles, we take a chance,
With wobbly grooves, we start to dance.

Bouncing balls in shades of fun,
Each juicy bite a happy pun.
As laughter spills, we can't resist,
A summer crush in fruity mist.

Tickles from the twiggy vines,
A jolly treat in sunny dines.
With every slice, a giggle pops,
In nature's game, no one stops!

Nature's Morning Mosaic

Colors burst in sunlight's gleam,
In the garden, we all dream.
Silly shapes in playful form,
Nature dresses, bright and warm.

Round and plump, they sway and roll,
Like little orbs that tease the soul.
With laughter shared, we take our seat,
For breakfast fun, it's quite the treat!

Birds take flight in lively arcs,
Casting shadows, tiny sparks.
Sweet and tart, they lift our mood,
With every slice, we're more subdued!

Ripe Reflections

In the dawn, a gleeful spot,
Reflecting joy, we laugh a lot.
Sliced delight, a funny sight,
Sipping juice till late at night.

A group of friends, all silly fun,
With smiles that shine like morning sun.
Belly laughs and sticky hands,
Creating joy in summertime lands.

Chasing crumbs beneath the shade,
Witty stories are displayed.
Oh, the giggles that we share,
Ripe reflections in the air!

Harvest of Colors

In tents of green with smiles so wide,
Laughter pops as fruit's kin hide.
Colors splash in big, round glee,
Nature's joke, a fruit jubilee.

We pluck them up, we toss around,
Their sweet giggles, a joyful sound.
Juicy dribbles, a sticky spree,
It's a party! Oh, come and see!

With every bite, we jump and cheer,
Squirrels dance; they've found their beer!
In fields so bright, we make a mess,
The funniest sight you'd ever guess!

So gather round, enjoy the fun,
A day of color, laughter won.
Let's fill our bellies, round and bold,
With nature's gifts, our hearts of gold.

Fields of Flavor

Beneath the sun, the treasure glows,
With silly hats and silly toes.
Each fruit a joke, a playful jest,
A harvest party, we are blessed!

The wind whispers secrets, a fruity chat,
While bees wear sunglasses; imagine that!
We roller-skate across the grass,
As water fights make sweet ones splash!

In flavors wild, we take a bite,
A comedy act with each delight.
Red and green, a circus show,
Where giggles bloom and sweet juice flows!

Come one, come all, to taste and cheer,
In fields of flavor, laughter's near.
A fruity feast, so loud and bright,
Let's dance around till day turns night!

Clarity of Dawn

Morning wakes in colors bold,
With fruity laughter, tales retold.
Sunrise smiles like a goofball,
Bringing joy with every call.

A breakfast spread, oh what a scene,
Honey and zest, a fruity queen.
With every slice, the day's a prank,
And juice spills out like a water tank!

Woeful squirrels, they fight in vain,
For fruity treats, we laugh, they feign.
There's blueberry pie and orange zest,
In dawn's embrace, we feel the best!

So take a seat, let's raise a toast,
To juicy chuckles and laughter most.
In clarity bright, we burst and bloom,
Fruity fun shall chase the gloom!

Sunlit Abundance

In rays of gold, the fruits appear,
Giggling softly, spreading cheer.
A basket full of happy munch,
We snack and giggle, it's a crunch!

With every bite, a joke unfolds,
Bananas slip; oh, laughter holds!
The sunlight dances on our face,
As we tumble in this tasty race!

Delightful friends in hats too wide,
Rolling down the hill with pride.
Sunlit abundance feels just right,
A fruity carnival, pure delight!

So grab a slice, come join the play,
In the warm glow of the day.
With juicy smiles that fill the air,
We celebrate this fruitful flair!

www.ingramcontent.com/pod-product-compliance
Lightning Source LLC
Chambersburg PA
CBHW060111230426
43661CB00003B/150